Help the squirrel find The acorns ?

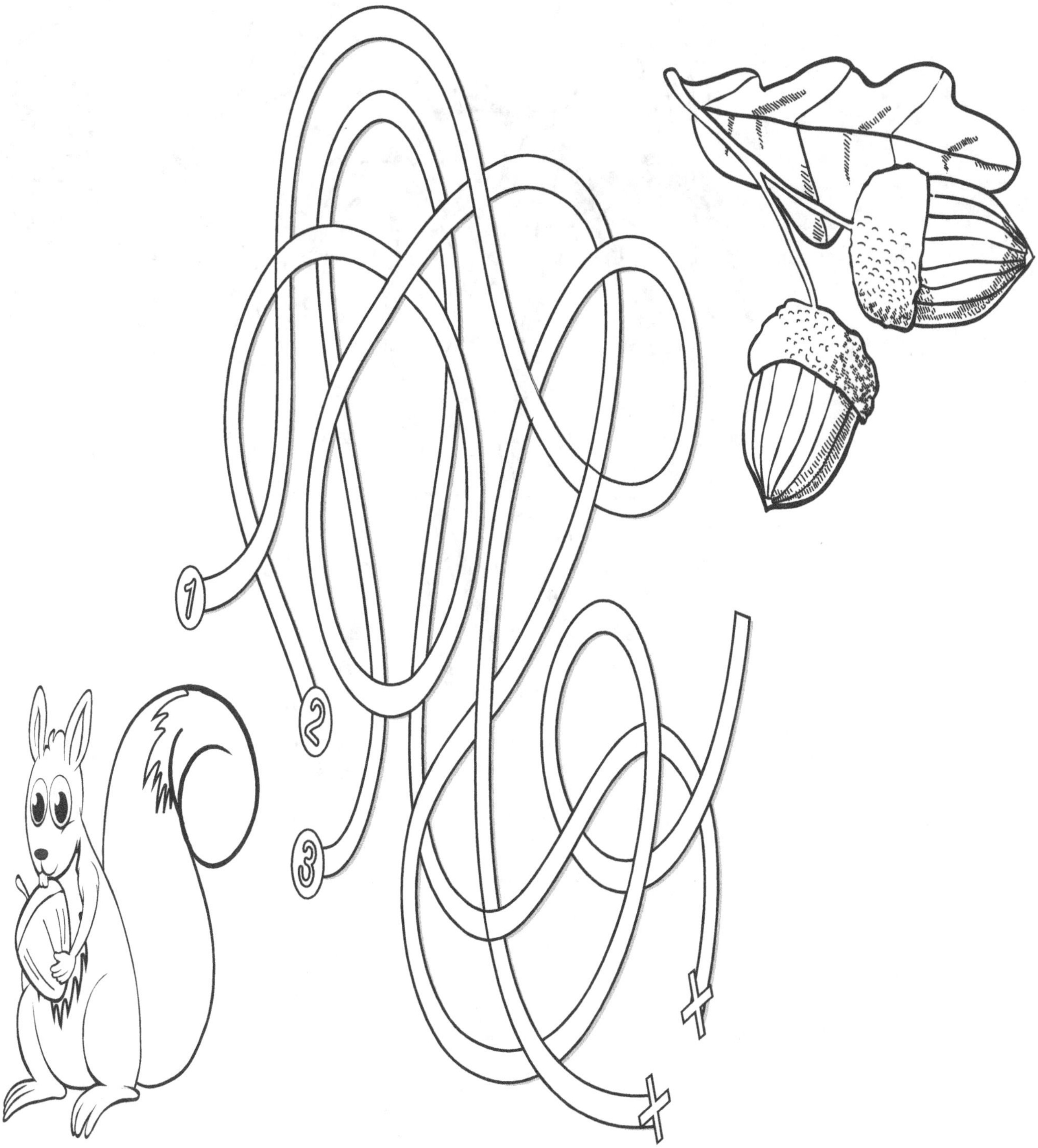

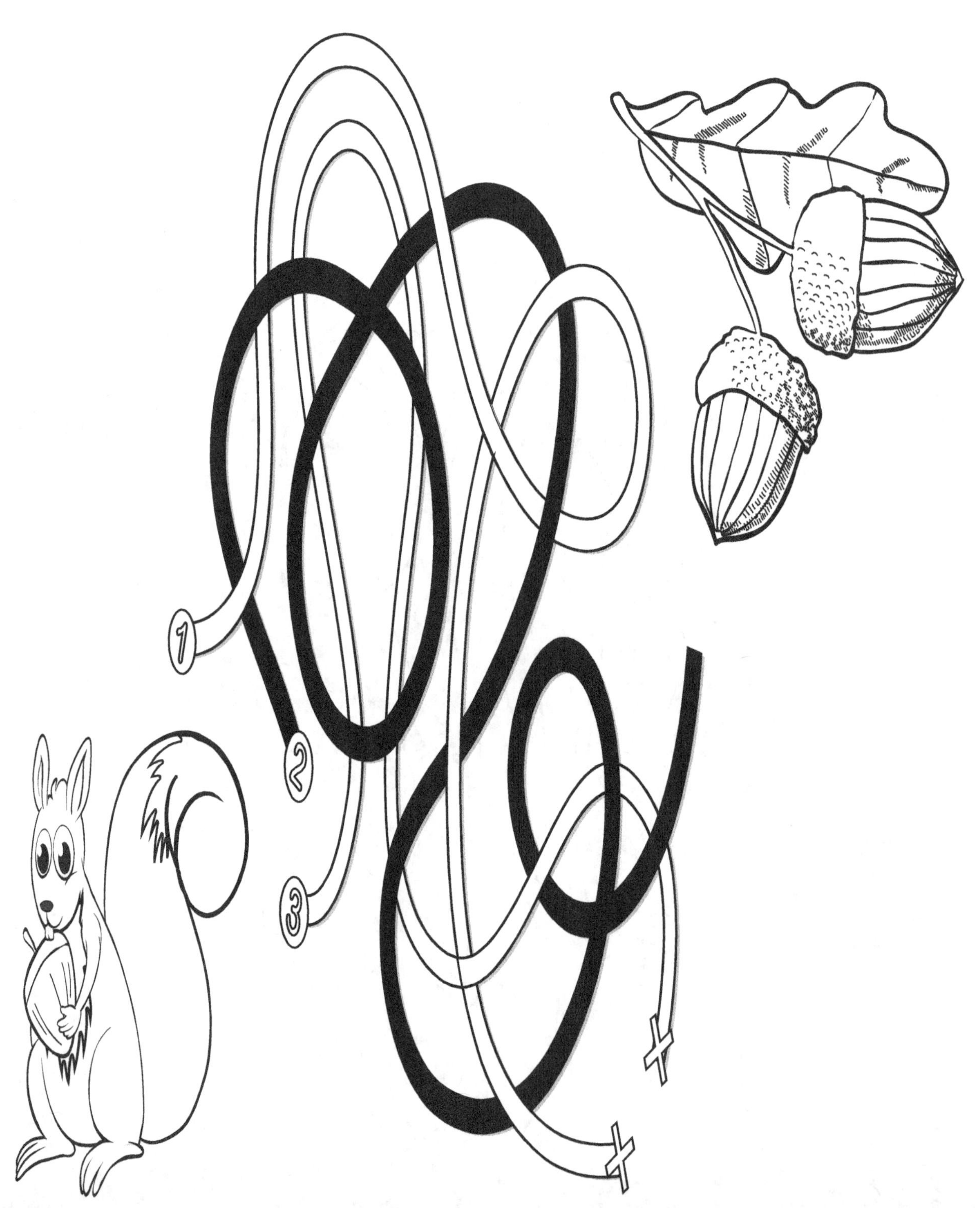

Help the kid find his candy

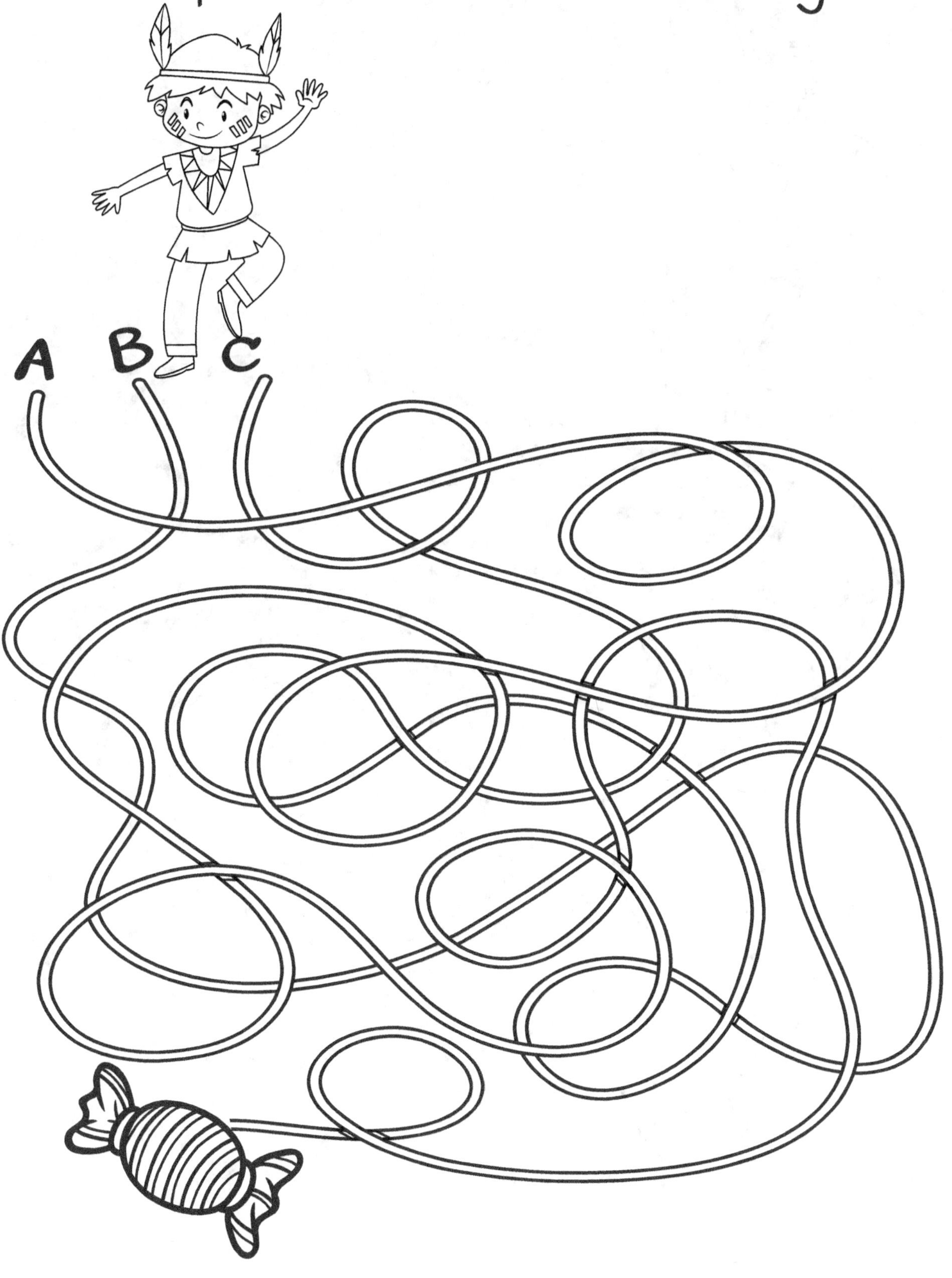

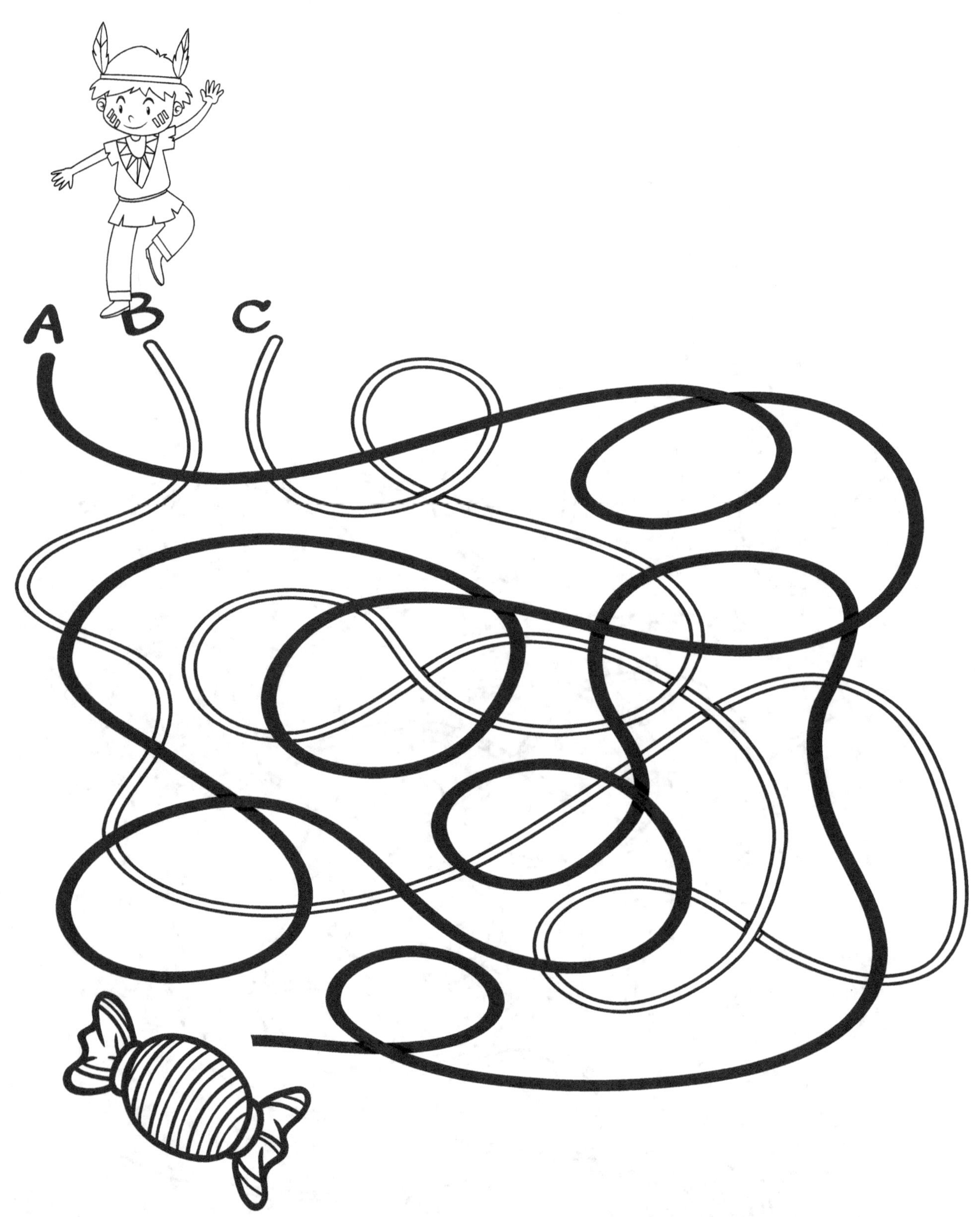
A
B
C

Find the pie

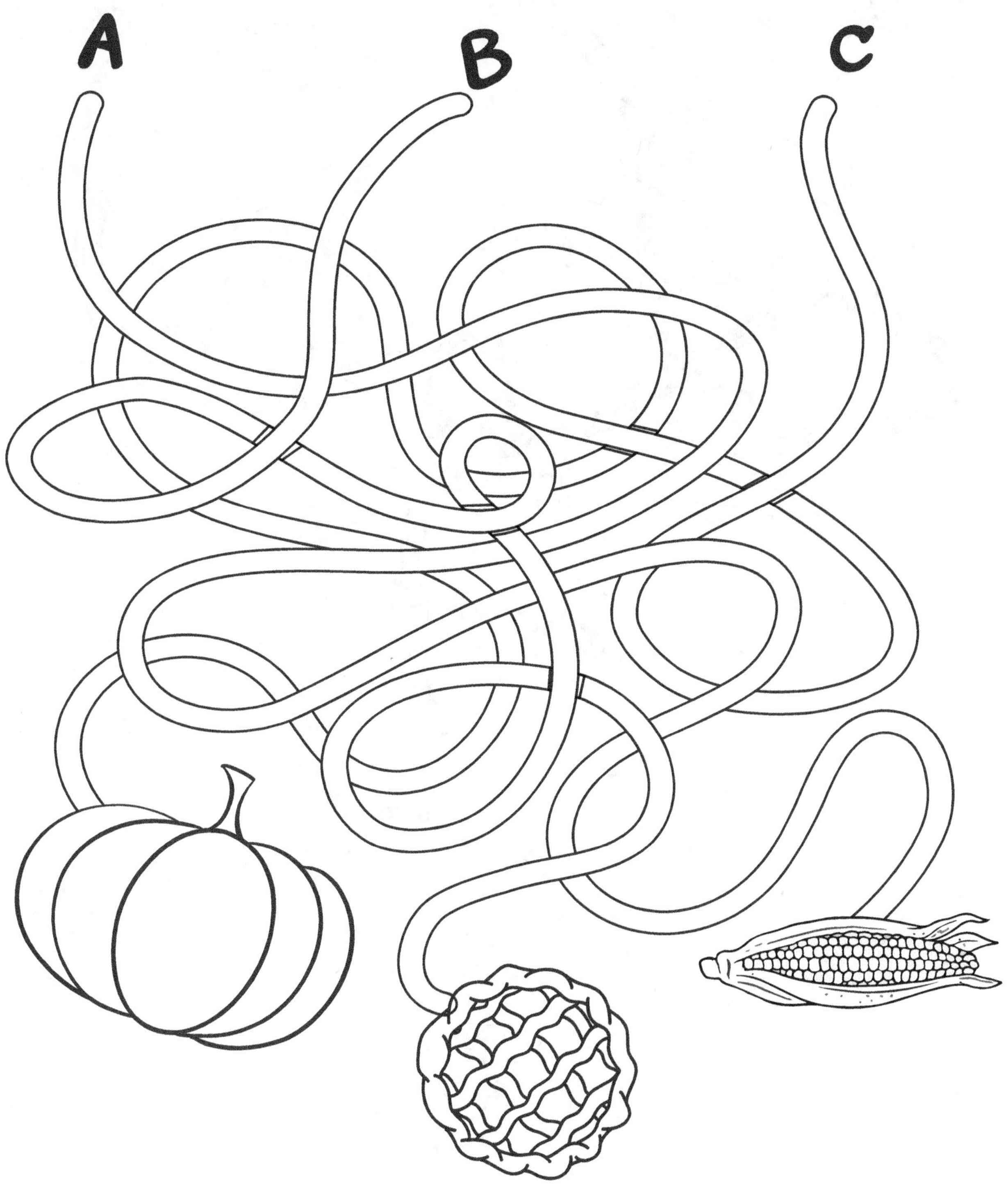

A
B
C

Help him find the wish bone

A
B
C
D
E

Help the rabbit find his home

Find the quince

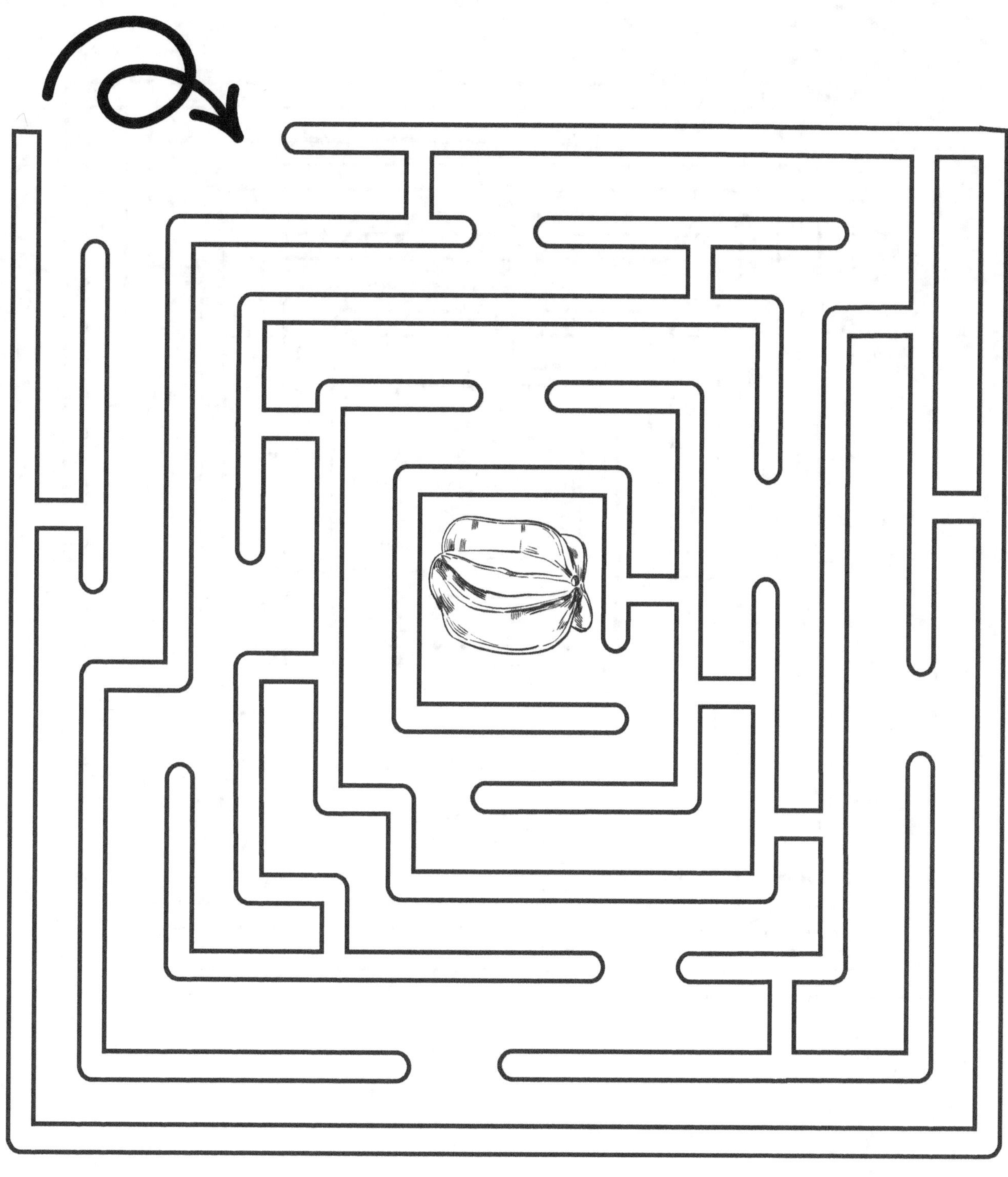

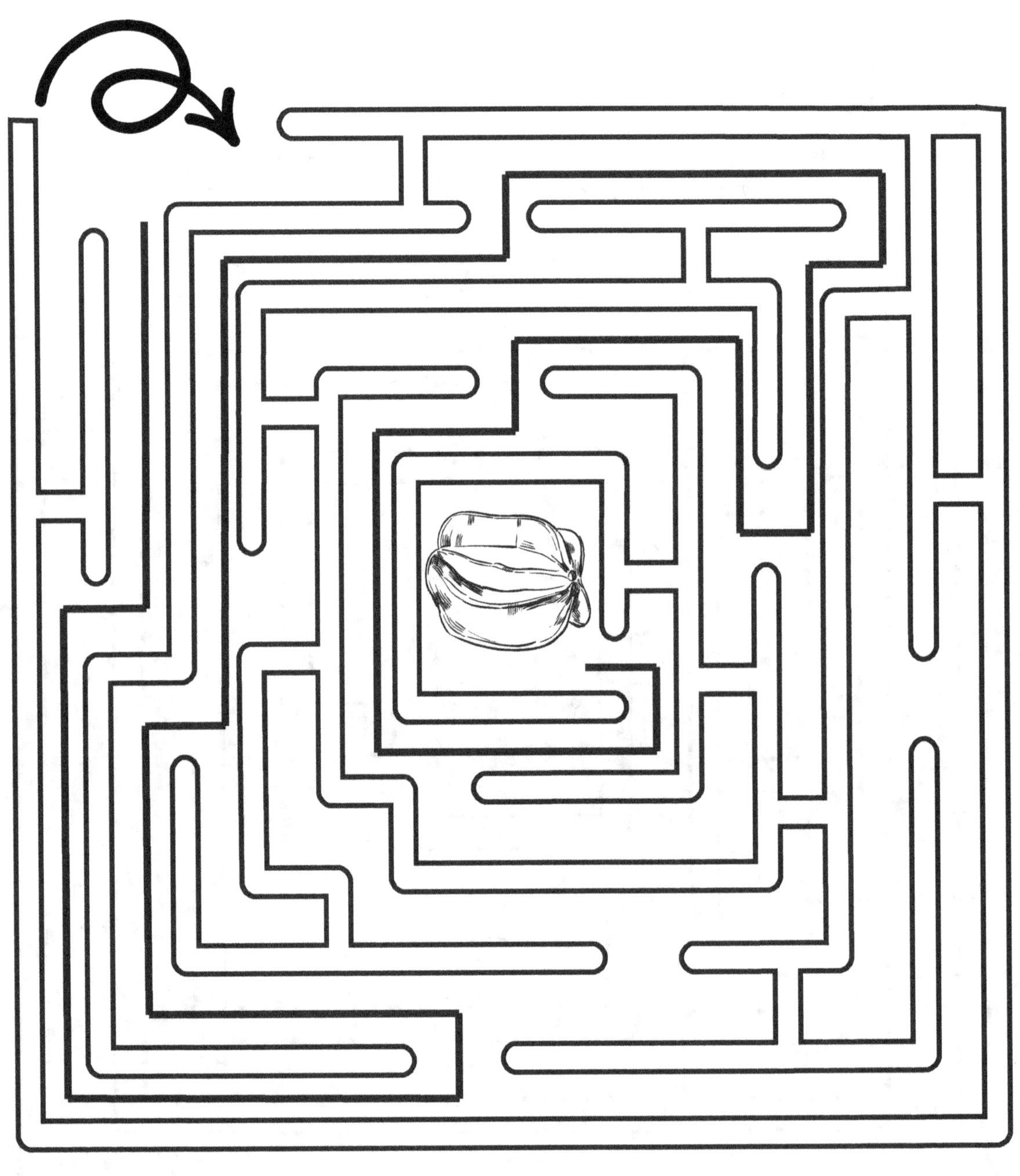

Find the delicious dish

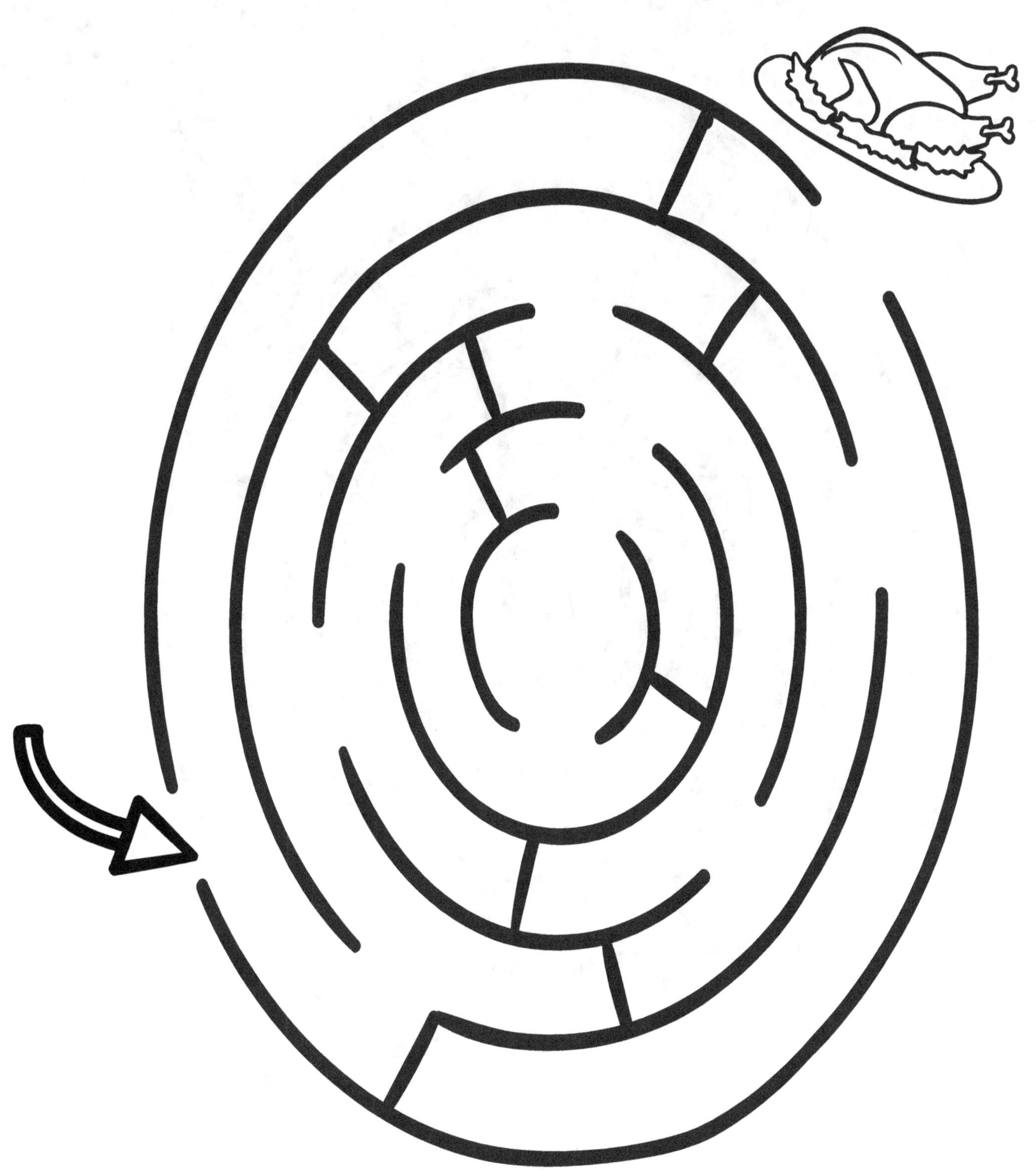

Find the object that starts with A

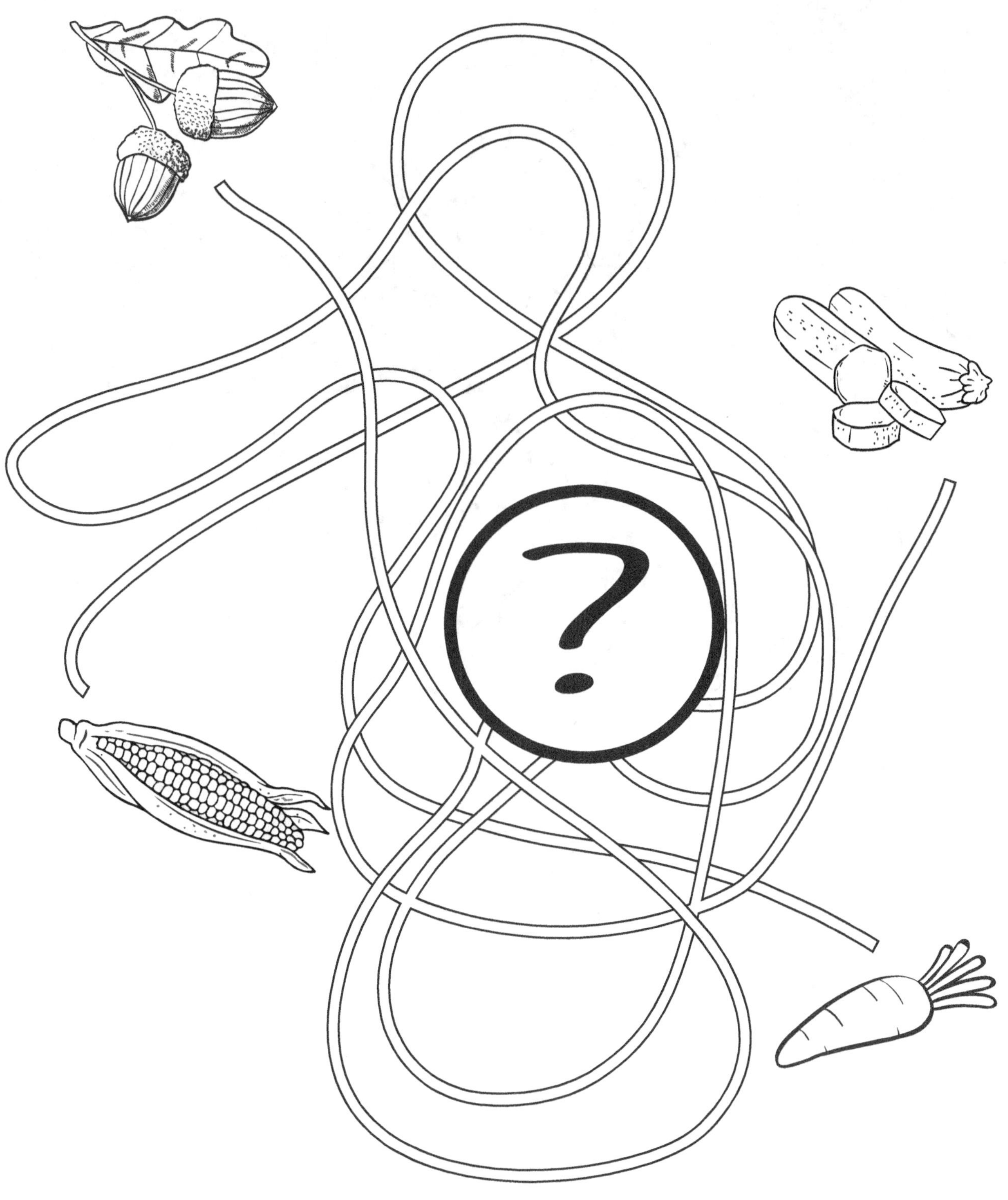

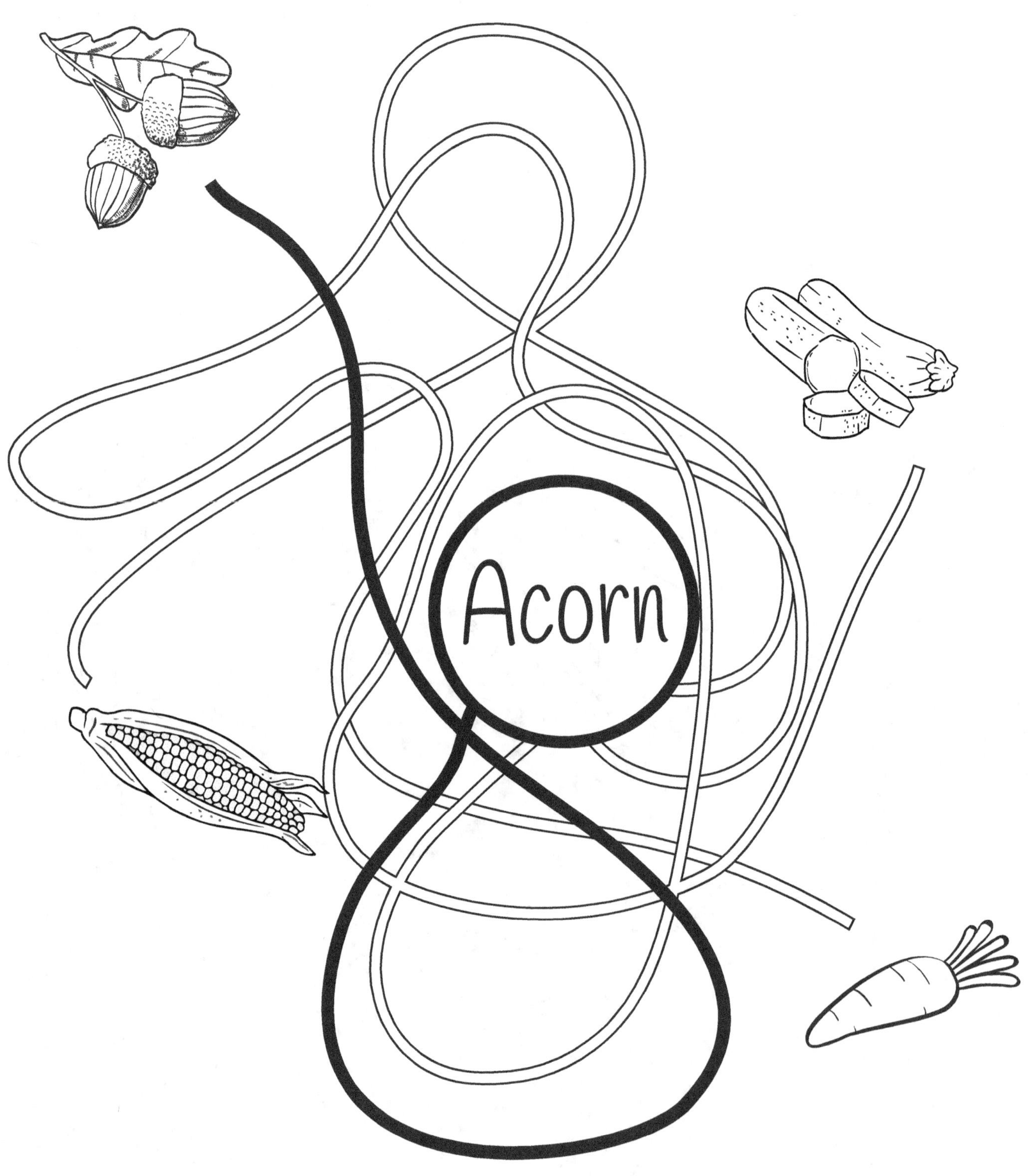
Acorn

Help granda find thanksgiving supper

Take the pie to the oven

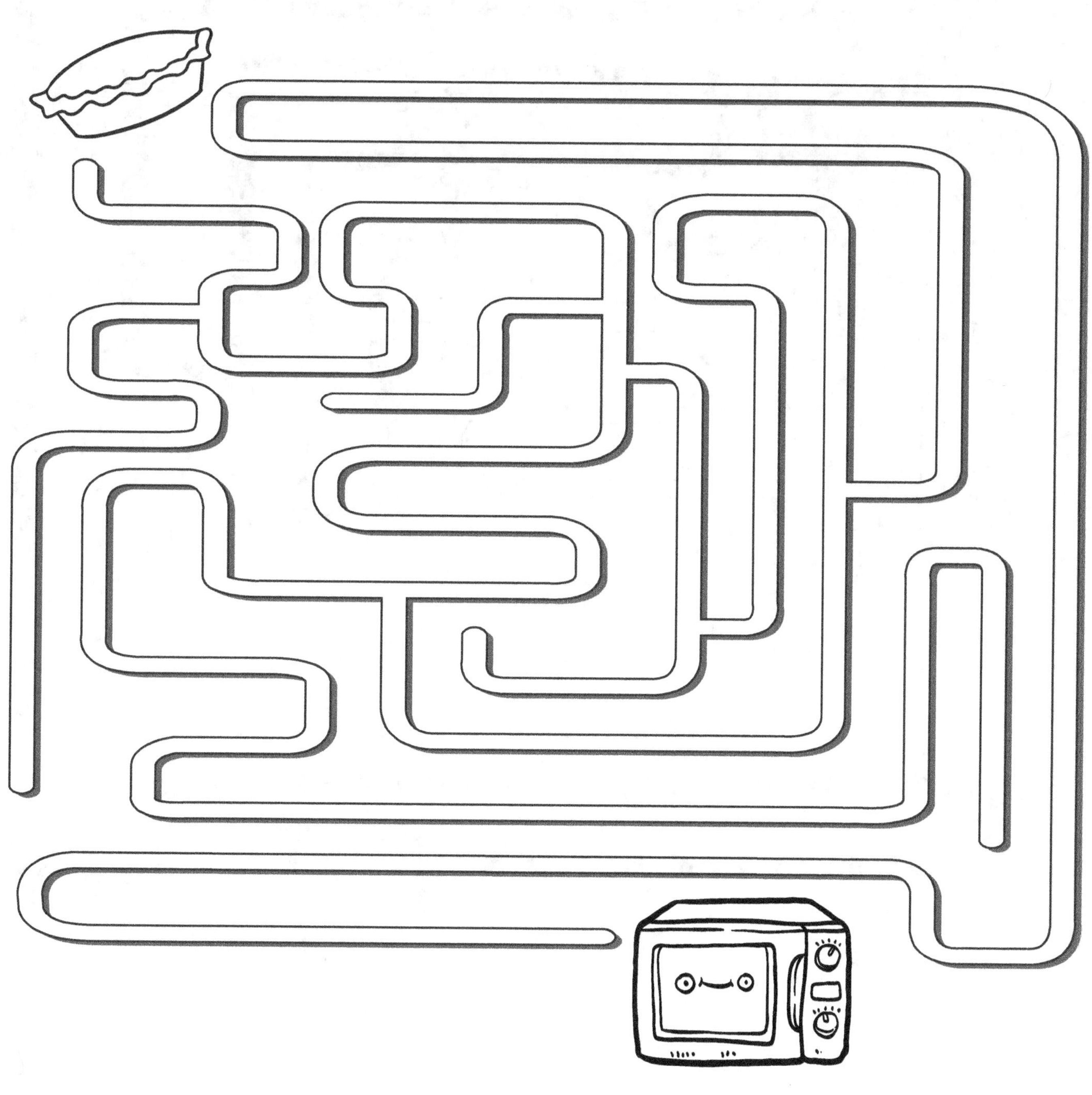

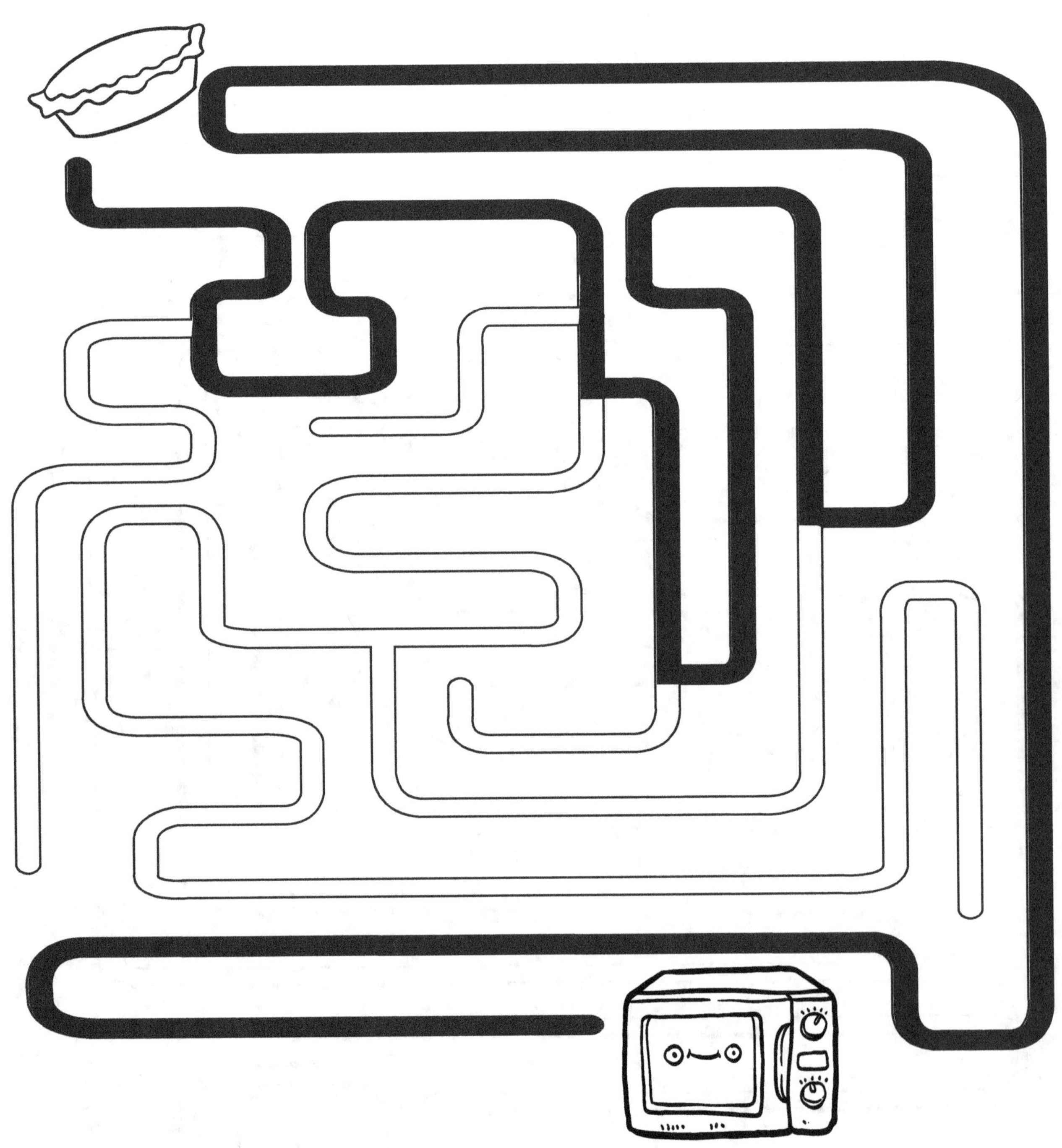

«THANKFUL» Tracing

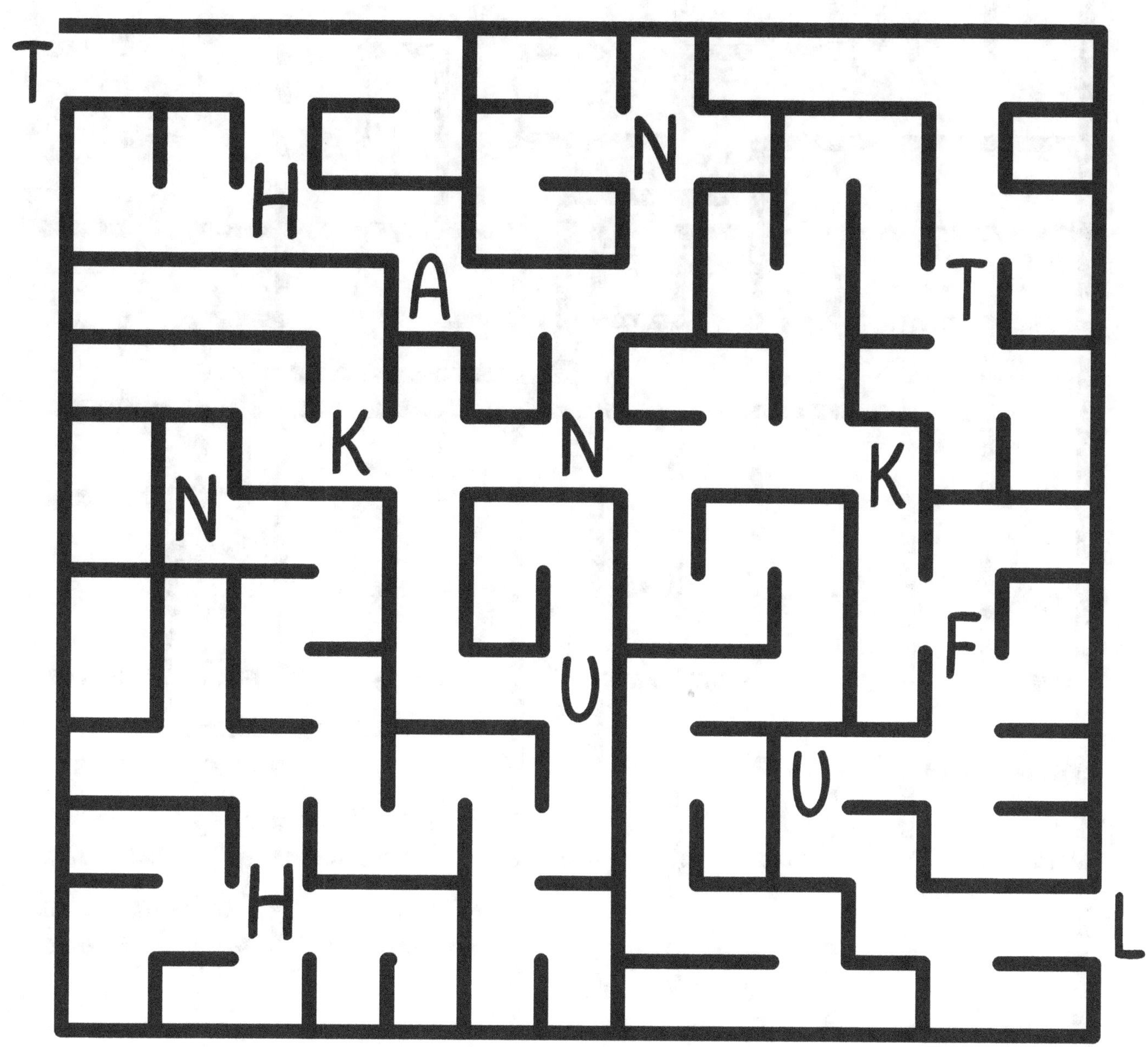

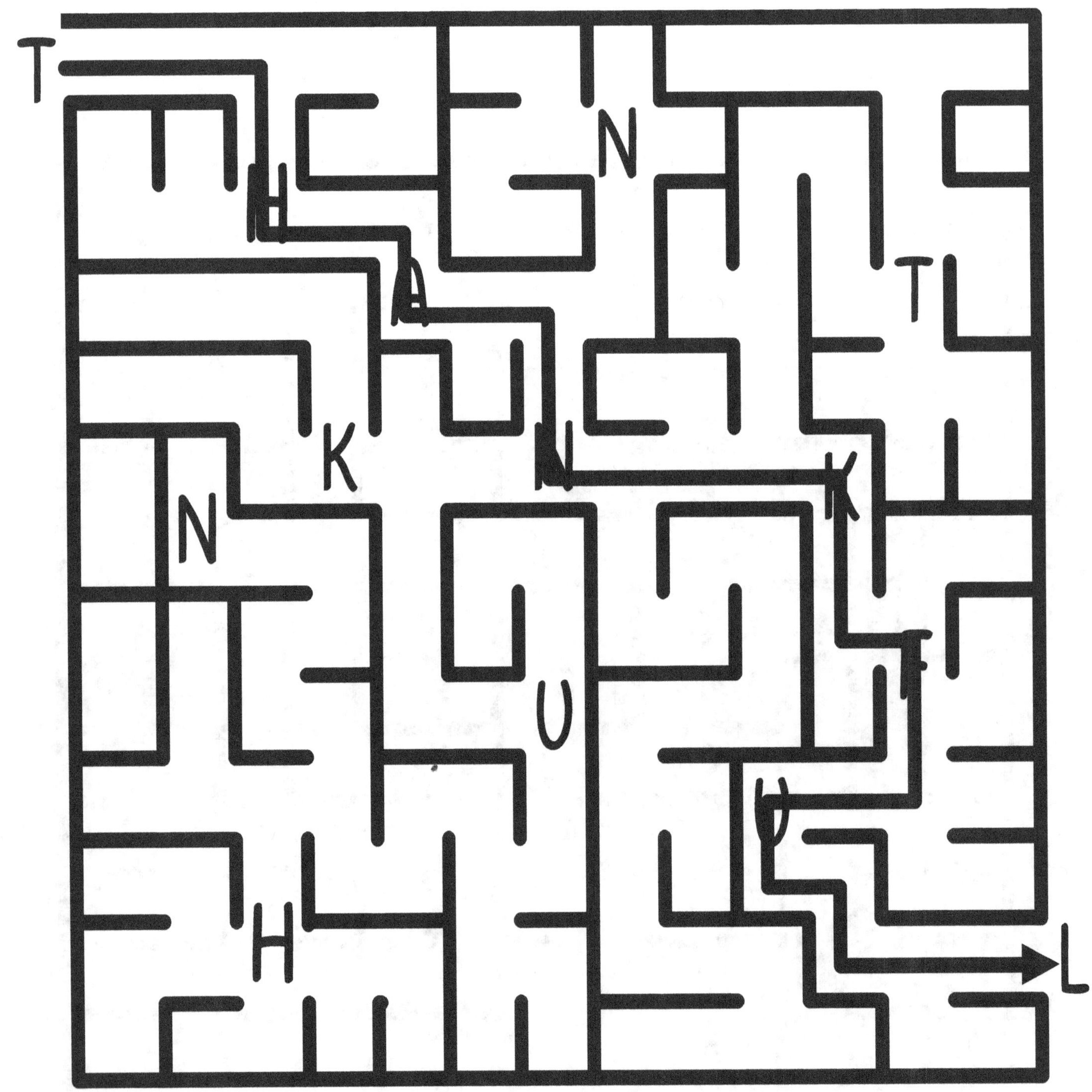

T
N
T
H
N
K
N
K
N
U
H
U
L

Take the duck out

Find the way out

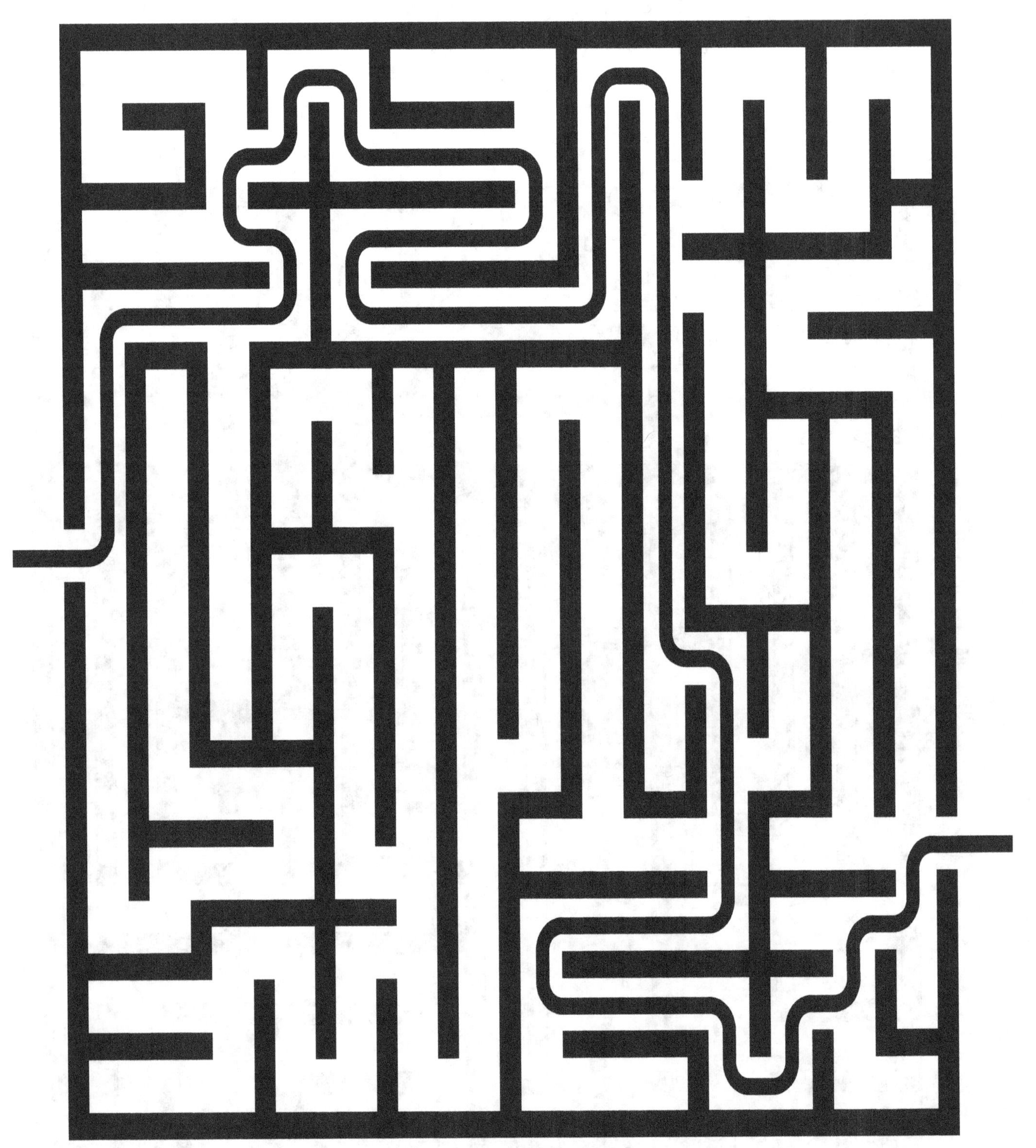

Find the vegetable that starts with Z

Zucchini

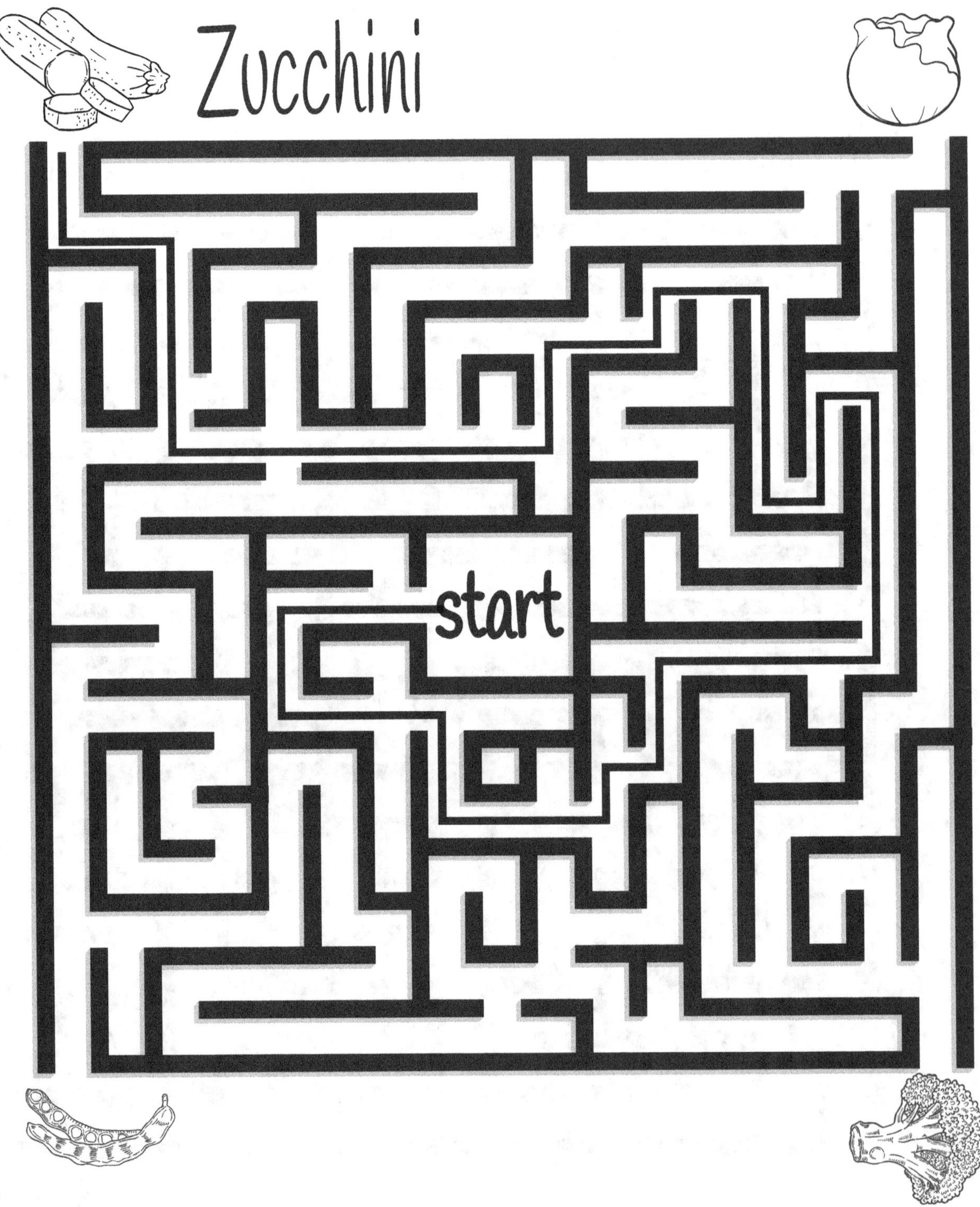

Help the squirrel find the way out